FORD

Daniel Gustafsson

MARBLE POETRY

Editor: Aisling Tempany

Marble Poetry

88 Pearl Street

Cardiff

CF24 1PL

www.marblepoetry.com

ISBN: 978-1-9163369-0-2

Set in Charis SIL

Printed by Mixam, Watford. Photo by Dave Clubb on Unsplash

HOLY ISLAND

Here

upon this no man's

island, holy ground

is all at sea. Came to this

by burning bridges; now

the bones of broken arches

hold our hearts from the deep.

SAGA

1

Scars and skerries recall it.

Say that he bore down
        from boreal climes,
a northerly wielding
        the keel-blade,
        surf-scatter strewn
in his wake.

Say that he captained
                an unearthly vessel;
say that he practised
            an unholy craft,
            carving his runes
with the strakes.

Turning the tide with his tiller,

seeding these shores with his prow.

2

Call him Halfdan,
whole-hearted halfwit,
heedlessly hell-bent on glory.

Say that he set sail for bounty;
say that he jumped ship for good.

3

Say he was there for the sacking;

swilling the lees

of the chalice,

staining the glass

with his look.

Say it was there

in the silenced chapel

he drew first blood

from the book.

Say that the cross-words confounded,

causing his crow's feet to fail;

say his barbed imagination

caught on the fisherman's hook.

4

Say he was there for the hacking;

hewing the groves
        into gallows,
grafting vines
        to ashen wood.
There, in the span
        of a speeding sparrow,
        blotting out
the raven's brood.

Say he suffered a change of art,
        saw the images altered,

saw his all-father orphaned there,
        strung from a branch of the rood.

5

Watch him, Halfdan

harrow of havens,

crossing the hilt of his hammer;

harper who strung up the hallows,

taking a new rune to heart.

6

Gathering tribute,

gathering forces,

two strands converge at the causeway.

Brackish the wound-sweat,

sweetened the saltings,

bitter the mingling of bloodlines.

Kinfolk on this bank,

fyrd on the further,

watch as he falters in fealty.

Say his *fylgia*

dove first: followed her

down like a dipper.

Say he was in it

over his head.

Scaling, salmon-wise and spotless,

crimson currents of his kind.

Consonant with cleaving waters,

confluent in forking tongues.

7

Call him turncoat,

shape-shifting sheepskin,

berserker bound for his bleating.

Say they stripped him

                    bare to birch-bole,

skin as Balder-bright as bone;

say they clothed him in pelts of stone.

8

Flowing furrows, recall him.

Bring us, burns,

his parting verses.

Bier him, becks,

to his berthing.

Cairns

on the cusp of the coursing,

stepping-stones

immersed in foam,

say

to those who would follow:

Sea-farer,

word-hoarder,

keeper of kennings,

follow this stave-bearer

into the spray.

Cross over,

sky-warder,

under the water,

follow this all-forder

into the fray.

ANGLE

Watching

the world at an angle,

under the fisherman's sign,

each thing inclines

to its likeness.

Birches

that bough down

to silver, tall reeds that taper

to gold. All is the making

of mirrors.

Lilies that paddle the cloudless,

herons that hover

below.

Watching this

is all I know. Stirrings

that ruffle the clean slate,

calm that restores it

to sky.

Two kingdoms come

here together. All things converge

at the crossing of lines.

WADERS

Ink on an old map
would bleed out like this, blotting
its outline of shore. So the river
brims its banks, laps up
the steps to the footpath, calling the bluff
on our gates. Makes a hurdle
of habit. Makes a quest of quotidian chores.
                    Waist-deep
in sludge on the flagstones
waders are forced now to wait here
or wing it. Must make do
with what's undone, must make other
ways across, other rights and wrongs
of passage, parting the upsurge of clay.
                    Rills of it,
forging their new blades, widen the range
of the breach, deepen the sense

of the cleaving. Two-edged
like all tongues, the sundering seam
channels the unsung deposits, stirs the remains
and the leavings. Uprooted
old barks, adrift on the current,
drag our dampened resolve in their wake.
                    And sirens,
intoning their cautions, say don't
get too close to get carried. Yet
dry bones are soaked through
to daring. Pent up
with toeing the shallows, fall forward
headfirst, for new kinds of footings,
grasping the sky for its give
and its take.

AFTER

Light now

the leafless and leaden.

Downstream

those levelled are upborne

again.

Mutely immersed yet

emerging as music, dry boughs

are dripping with spray.

REEDS

A dimple of light
in the blank slate, then
the beginnings of outlines
and hues. Lithely the reeds
are distinguished. Wavelets
and leaves overlapping, cyan from cobalt
unfurling its plumes, they dance
at your delicate summons, drawn
out of dimness to dazzle
in you.

So, through the medium
of your love, my world is held up
to wonder. Glorying here in your gaze,
banners of gold interlacing
rise from this lakewater study
in blue.

POSY

Picked

in the glare and the gusts

of the roadside, poised now

like paints on a palette. No less

alive for their stillness, no less

themselves in this new composition,

sunlight still stalks them

inside.

Later,

leafing through the flora,

training lips to frame the forms

of unfamiliar names – *rödklöver,*

stjärnflocka, ängsskära,

blåklocka – something is gained

in translation.

Even at dawn

undiminished, each petal

yet more defined now, each line

distinct as if carved

out of time.

CARGO

Sea-change

relies on the ferryman's art:

unmooring one ship to berth

with another. So, as the heart's compass

wings round again, wheels

like a crane for the far shores,

keepsakes are best left

to breakers: crates overturned

on the bare rocks, old bottles bursting

with brine.

                Hauled overseas

under wrappings, beached

at the end of the whale-road

lids come unsealed to the light.

Here, as we pick up the pieces

together, unsheathed like pearls

from their trappings, life seems the greater

for shedding some parts.

Such are the same objects'

altering powers, these things I called mine

now answer to ours.

DIVININGS

1

Tongues uprooted
from local springs,
we have lost the words
for thirst. Baked clay
this dry spell is ours
for the breaking.
                    Language,
a hard crust that longs
for the quaking, calls us
to sharpen the tools.
Digging down
with rod and auger, drill
for the water that wells
in the wounds.

2

The quiet lake
an open page. Sit here
sounding the silence,
putting your love on the line.
                Watch
the quivering rod relay
the indiscernible life.
                Here,
where silence becomes us,
where language is all
and in all, hear the water-
words that are
before the water
was.

THE ALWAYS MOOR

1

Leave the city
by kissing gates.
Here where the ring-road
devours its tail,
tar at the end of its tether,
hawthorn and heather
will pick up the trail.

Follow a red thread
that runs here:
fuses the rowan and rosehip,
flares in fireweed and ferns.
Then, as purple swards unfurl,
follow the ribbon of limestone,
leading light on this royal floor.

2

While daylight
frays on the brambles,
flags our rovings and rambles,
take the wind's unbridled way –
on paths less trampled
by paraphrase.

From the stream,
a lucent bed,
rise to find the fountainhead
forcing the rock face above:
see it leap
from crag to cove,
sheering the side of the fell.
Go to fill your cup with this –
the plenitude,
the always pour.

3

Climb
the ladders of slate,
layers that greyscale the landscape;
scramble the scree slope
to stagger the view:
patchwork of drystone and pasture,
kestrels that cross-stitch
the torn strips of blue.
Watch for the cloudbank to sunder:

come-down of light
on the uplands,
gleaming on glitters and gills.
Breathless here
on this narrow sill,
stand back to bird-eye
the wonder.

THE BURIED SHIP

Right here
the keel's wedge was driven;
here, where the moorlands
were riven with light, mark now
the grooves of its graving,
prowing the limestone and loam.
                    Still the bark
lies buried here, wrecked
on the bulwark of bracken,
gunwales engulfed now by gorse.
Craft of our foundered fathers,
landlocked from lippers and foam.
                    A reliquary
of dying arts, reckoned
unsuited for service, stones
still circle the vacant helm,
a vast hull still hollows the barrow.

                    Still, though
rafters are bare, let us repair
to these ruins, make of this ramshackle
ship-shape a home. Come here,
castaways, as stewards,
stubbornly setting the thwart-boards
in line. Rig up your staves
for a scaffold; kneel down
where speedwells aspire.
                    Spurning back
with faces leeward, shore up
the shanties and sea-words;
chant response to the guttering
stars. Pray, though
pruning prevails now, saplings
may steeple this clearing with spars,
main-mast emerge from the mire.

STEPPING STONES

Go back
over the same grounds
again. Making amens
of your missteps, retrace
these ruts to the new.
Though these currents
have altered all,
still this passing place
remains.
                                        Go on,
step into it twice,
out of what was once
yourself. Letting go
of what was held then, let us
upend what we started.

Acknowledgements

Individual poems have previously appeared in *Dream Catcher*, *Eborakon*, *Marble*, *Pennine Platform*, and *The Lake*. My sincere thanks to the editors.